Contents

KU-706-582

Some words are shown in bold, **like this**. They are explained in the glossary on page 23.

What is embarrassment?

Embarrassment is a **feeling**. Feelings are something you feel inside. Everyone has different feelings all the time.

sad

happy

jealous

Feelings

WITHDRAWN FROM STOCK

Embarrassed

Sarah Medina

Illustrated by Jo Brooker

www.raintreepublishers.co.uk
Visit our website to find out more information about **Raintree** books.

To order:
☎ Phone 44 (0) 1865 888112
🖹 Send a fax to 44 (0) 1865 314091
🖥 Visit the Raintree Bookshop at **www.raintreepublishers.co.uk** to browse our catalogue and order online.

First published in Great Britain by Raintree, Halley Court, Jordan Hill, Oxford OX2 8EJ, part of Harcourt Education.
Raintree is a registered trademark of Harcourt Education Ltd.

© Harcourt Education Ltd 2008
First published in paperback in 2008
The moral right of the proprietor has been asserted.

All rights reserved. No part of this publication may be reproduced, stored in a retrieval system, or transmitted in any form or by any means, electronic, mechanical, photocopying, recording, or otherwise, without either the prior written permission of the publishers or a licence permitting restricted copying in the United Kingdom issued by the Copyright Licensing Agency Ltd, 90 Tottenham Court Road, London W1T 4LP (www.cla.co.uk).

Editorial: Diyan Leake and Cassie Mayer
Design: Joanna Hinton-Malivoire
Illustrations: Jo Brooker
Picture research: Erica Martin
Production: Duncan Gilbert

Originated by Dot Gradations
Printed and bound in China by
  South China Printing Company

ISBN 978 1 4062 0779 8 (hardback)
12 11 10 09 08
10 9 8 7 6 5 4 3 2 1

ISBN 978 1 4062 0786 6 (paperback)
13 12 11 10 09 08
10 9 8 7 6 5 4 3 2 1

British Library Cataloguing in Publication Data
Medina, Sarah
  Embarrassed. - (Feelings)
  1. Embarrassment - Juvenile literature
  I. Title
  152.4

Acknowledgements
The publishers would like to thank the following for permission to reproduce photographs:
Bananastock p. **22A, B, C**; Istrock/Slobo p. **22D**.

Every effort has been made to contact copyright holders of any material reproduced in this book. Any omissions will be rectified in subsequent printings if notice is given to the publishers.

3580728
Leabharlann
Chontae na Mídhe

When you feel embarrassed, you are uncomfortable in front of other people.

What happens when I feel embarrassed?

When you are embarrassed, you may feel hot and turn red. You might even feel like crying.

You may find it hard to talk to people, because you think that you might say something silly.

Why do I get embarrassed?

You might get embarrassed if lots of people are looking at you.

If someone **teases** you or laughs at you, you may feel embarrassed.

Is it OK to feel embarrassed?

Everybody feels embarrassed sometimes. Embarrassment is normal.

If you are embarrassed, people will usually understand and try to help you to feel better.

What can I do if I feel embarrassed?

If you feel embarrassed, tell someone who cares about you. They will help you.

Embarrassment may make you feel like hiding. Remember that things are never as bad as you think.

Will I always feel embarrassed?

It is normal for **feelings** to come and go. You will not always feel embarrassed.

When you are embarrassed, it may feel bad, but it does not last for long. You will soon feel better.

How can I tell if someone is embarrassed?

When others are embarrassed, they may not want to talk. They may want to be alone.

They may cover their face. Or they might not be able to keep still.

Can I help when someone is embarrassed?

You can help people when they are embarrassed. Be nice to them and never laugh at them.

Let them know that you like them
and that you want to be their friend.

Am I the only one to be embarrassed?

Remember, everyone feels embarrassed sometimes. Embarrassment is a very normal **feeling.**

It is good to know what to do when you feel embarrassed. That way, you can help yourself and other people!

Leabharlann
3580728
Contae na Mídhe

What are these feelings?

A

B

C

D

Which of these people looks embarrassed?

What are the other people feeling?

Look at page 24 for the answers.

Picture glossary

feeling
something that you feel inside. Embarrassment is a feeling.

tease
say something unkind, either as a joke or to upset someone

uncomfortable
not feeling good

Index

Answers to the questions on page 22
The person in picture D could be embarrassed.
The other people could be angry, proud, or caring.

Note to Parents and Teachers
Reading for information is an important part of a child's literacy development. Learning begins with a question about something. Help children think of themselves as investigators and researchers by encouraging their questions about the world around them. Most chapters in this book begin with a question. Read the question together. Look at the pictures. Talk about what you think the answer might be. Then read the text to find out if your predictions were correct. Think of other questions you could ask about the topic, and discuss where you might find the answers. Assist children in using the picture glossary and the index to practice new vocabulary and research skills.